Going Farther into the Woods than the Woods Go

MERCER
UNIVERSITY PRESS

Endowed by
TOM WATSON BROWN
and
THE WATSON-BROWN FOUNDATION, INC.

Going Farther into the Woods than the Woods Go

SEABORN JONES

MERCER UNIVERSITY PRESS
MACON, GEORGIA

MUP/P443

© 2011 Seaborn Jones
Published by Mercer University Press
1400 Coleman Avenue
Macon, Georgia 31207

First Edition

Books published by Mercer University Press are printed on acid-free paper that meets the requirements of American National Standard for Information Sciences—Permanence of Paper for Printed Library Materials.

Mercer University Press is a member of Green Press Initiative (greenpressinitiative.org), a nonprofit organization working to help publishers and printers increase their use of recycled paper and decrease their use of fiber derived from endangered forests. This book is printed on recycled paper.
ISBN   978-0-88146-272-2
Cataloging-in-Publication Data is available from the Library of Congress

For

Raeder, Denny, Bronwyn, Scott

Barbara Ann Thornton

Pat Landreth Keller, Mark Keller

Acknowledgments

Chattahoochee Review, "The Drought"; *PoetryNZ*, "Berlin"; *Rockhurst Review*, "The Endeavor" and "Becoming an Artist"; *Wilshire Review*, "Do Not Read this Poem Until You Have Finished Reading It" and "Without a License"; *Heeltap*, "Work" and "Stalking the Predator"; *Southern Poetry Review*, "Solstice"; *Louisiana Review*, "All My Life," "The Fly," and "Looking for a Safe Place to Die"; *Chiron Review*, "Refugees," "Communiqué," "After the Liberation," "The Election," and "Directions"; *Java Monkey Speaks Anthology*, Volume Three, "Going Farther into the Woods than the Woods Go"; *J Journal*, "Virtual Lack of Reality"; and *Art Life*, "Today" and "Which Way."

CONTENTS

I.

My Life Is a Getaway Car in Reverse

The weather runs a fever. Triple-digit moons.
I'm equatorially confused. My hair is already dead.
Road rage in the kitchen. Serrated verbs.
Concentric voices. Double-barrel blue eyes.
A smile showing too many teeth. Traffic-light lipstick.
A recurring dream that's never the same.
Haunted by wordless thoughts. Curriculum of fears.
Medication vs. meditation. Music is emergency.
Chain gang smoke bang. High-speed oven on bridge's curve.
The alarm clock speedometer hits ninety.
My mind strips gears. Coffee and gasoline.
My nails are dead but painted and growing still.
Memory disappears through libido's trapdoor.
The future always repeats itself.

Looking for a Safe Place to Die

The alarm clock, telephone, and doorbell ring
at the same time. Day breaks like glass.
Shark fins emerge through the floor.
I'm in love with fear.
In the underground altitudes, who are you?
Is this the emergency room or the kitchen?

The electric burner's concentric coils
are the Devil's four hot eyes.
Here's the earring you thought you lost forever;
I found it under the mat where
I thought I lost my mind.

This must be the I.V. umbilical cord that
connects me to myself. A shadow of something,
either dancing or dying, crosses the wall.
My fingers are candles that will not blow out.
I feel like a fool for having made so many wishes.
Neon x-rays exit freeways where
skid marks disappear into the heart.

Why Listen to Strangers When You Can Listen to Me? I'm Stranger Than Anybody

I feel too close to myself.
I spend too much time
minding my own business
instead of meddling
in other people's lives.
I spread treacherous rumors
about myself. I leave threatening
messages on my answering machine.
I need the courage to
upset other people
instead of myself.
I need myself as a friend
and at this age
it seems like I would be someone
I could turn to,
but the face in the mirror says,
"You have come too close,
back off, you better
find somebody else to mess with."

The Endeavor

Going through my
wardrobe of skulls
I find an
animated anima,
a lidless id,
a libido hitchhiking
on a curve, my shadow
beating its fists
against a lace wall.
It's a recurring dream
that interprets me
like a row of old men
watching the sea
through mandala portholes.
I'm passing it back
through my ancestors
generation by generation
to the first
instant of time.
It's the dream that says,
"Open your mouth;
I am the
French kiss of death."

Work

Each morning
I fit my body
like a jigsaw
puzzle, piece
by reluctant
piece, into
the world where
facedown on
the floor to
flex my back then
up on my hands
and knees
I stretch to
my feet like
evolution
an upright step
toward the invisible
predator we call
pain.

The Drought

I'm tired of the relentless blue sky,
the perfect circle of yellow sun
that says, "Smile, be happy like me."
Not to mention the woman in the waiting room
telling her daughter to "be the best that she can be."

I'm tired of waiting for the doctor
to tell me that I don't hurt, waiting for
red circles to turn green, stopping when
it's time to stop, going when
it's time to go, arriving when
it's time to arrive.

The clock says, "Sleep."
The light says, "Turn me off."
The pillow says, "Turn me over."
The sheet says, "Pull me down."
The clock says, "Wake."

I don't want to smile, be happy, wait, hurt, wait, stop,
go, arrive, sleep, turn, turn, pull, wake.

I don't even want to "be the best that I can be."
I want to be God so I can bring a safe, gray sky
that holds soft rain until
a crescent moon says, "I, too, am tired."

Solstice

The world is turning
into winter and
I am a winter man.

Winter is moving toward us
through the trees and
I am a tree man.

Winter is falling from
the sky and
I am a sky man.

Winter is changing rain
into ice and
I am an ice man.

Winter is shooting silver
into stars and
I am a star man.

Winter is releasing the wind
from its cage and
I am a cage man.

Black and White

If I woke
unsure whether it were
afternoon or morning
and there
at the foot of the bed
a boy without blue eyes
tossing apples
into the air
and with a bullwhip
cracking them
into perfect halves—
an old rodeo movie
to carry
like a secret
into the oncoming
night or day.

The Cherry Blossom Festival

The pink pancakes are on a rotating grill.
It's imperative that I get an exact count.
The rotating pink pancakes are on television,
a Cherry Blossom Festival (If it were Saint Patrick's Day, the
pancakes would be green.).

Segue to the weather, a possibility of rain; then
the news, a man in the Middle East waving an AK-47
over his head; a commercial, someone selling
furniture, Big-Boy recliners, patio features;
another commercial, someone selling zirconium pendants,
Limited Edition.

It's too early in the morning to discuss the genesis of the psyche,
hereditary information in the brain stem,
the reptile sleeping inside us, or
the frontal lobe, a planet
inside a skull.

I should shave and shower but the fate of the universe
depends on the number of slats in the Venetian blinds,
counting and recounting windowpanes,
washing and rewashing hands.
The rituals of blessing inanimate objects,
locking and relocking doors,
counting and recounting the sun
to make sure it hasn't multiplied.

And who knows, this homemade numerology
could prevent diseases from colliding with comets.

Now the commentator says,
"Well, it looks like you finished your plate,"

and the overweight man in the John Deere T-shirt answers,
"Yes, I did,"
and the woman beside him in the pink hat (if it were
Saint Patrick's Day, the hat would be green) says,
"It was good."

But how many pancakes did they eat?
The commentator failed to ask.
The world will never know.
The man on the Gaza Strip will continue firing his AK-47
into the air,
the sum of the bullets
added to the sum of the pancakes while
reptiles and planets subtract themselves from color.

Maybe Tomorrow

Hoping absence
will make the heart
grow fonder

I've gone for days
without looking
in a mirror

but shake my head
refuse eye contact
walk away.

All My Life

All mirrors agree that I am worthless.
They conspire to shatter and cut me to pieces.

I lock them in closets when I sleep.
I dig holes and bury them in the backyard;
I shovel dirt on my faces of fear.

Mirrors have followed me all of my life.
They have hunted me down, surprised me
in restaurants, hospitals, bus stations, airports,
hotels where no one spoke the same language.

And just this morning, the mirror in the hall
caught me off guard, confused and foolish.
I will seal it behind the walls where
I have disposed of many other mirrors.

Finding One's Self

I have a bone
to pick

with myself
and when

and if
I ever

find myself
I'm

going to
give myself

a piece of
my mind.

And Just Last Week

my doctor told me
the human head
weighs ten pounds,
the heaviness
of a bowling ball;
no wonder it's hard
to hold high,
tilt back
to see the stars,
or bury
in worried hands.

Hereditary One-Way Ticket

My death will come and come
slowly
like being trapped on an endless bus trip
with everyone singing
"ninety-nine bottles of beer
on the wall
if one of those bottles
should happen to
fall
there would be only
ninety-eight bottles of beer
on the wall."
Down to three bottles, two bottles,
one.
Then they start all over again from the top,
"ninety-nine bottles, ninety-eight..."
Too fast on slick roads, curves,
the bus rocking and leaning
side to side,
cliffs overlooking an abyss
of the Circus Maximus
and everyone singing as if nothing were wrong,
dancing in the aisles
to this mathematical excuse for a song,
this endless falling and subtracting,
this endless sound of breaking glass
while I roll on the floor
conjugating ancient fevers.

Holding a Séance for Myself Before I Die

Squeaking doors and swaying chandeliers
precede my appearance. Then
the room goes dark, except for my face
lit by a flashlight beneath my chin.
My parents gasp; my children weep.

I take a seat at the table where they wait.
I tap my finger once for "yes," twice for "no."

They ask if I have money. I tap twice.
They sigh with disgust.
They ask if I'm returning permanently. I tap twice.
They sigh with relief.

I whisper, "I love you. I love you."
Their chairs squeak like doors. They sway like chandeliers.
They may even remember I'm not dead yet.

Becoming an Artist

I always heard that artists became immortal
so I became an artist.

Only thing is

I thought people were saying *immoral*, not *immortal*,
that if I were an artist I could be immoral
and even have the power, through my work,
to make others immoral.

I don't want to live forever.

The Verge of Saying

All my life I've been on a blind date with myself,
not sure what to wear, what to expect, what to say…

unsure in a world of high fashion,
designer landscapes, designer sunsets,
sky with matching water, trees with matching grass,

and me with my simple clothing
woven from the hair of my enemies;

my humble shelter, a cabin
made from the bones of my friends and family;

my table set with chopsticks and painted skulls
filled with rice and feathers;

my limited vocabulary, consisting of only one word—
a word I can't ever remember, but am always on
the verge of saying.

Without a License

I control the angle of the stars
as they rise from the
skyline of the city that
comes closer after driving
too long. The rearview mirror
fills with intentional accidents.
It seems the faster I drive
the closer the windshield should come.

I'm driving toward your house.
I've been driving for a long time.
Since the day you were born.
I'm almost there. Be ready to go.
All you'll need is perfume and a knife.
We'll follow the light of the
dial on the radio.

Berlin

This is Berlin. I'm holding it
between my thumb and index finger;
a sugar cube, white, like snow.
At least I call it Berlin.
If I had two sugar cubes
I could have two Berlins, but
for now: one Berlin.

I've never been to Berlin but
I imagine someone in Berlin a long time ago,
holding a sugar cube over a cup of tea
just as I'm doing, watching the snow fall
outside a window, a wife waiting for
her husband to return from war, a soldier
waiting to go to war, a child
putting the cube into her mouth
instead of into the tea.

Freud or Chagall in a café or studio,
each looking at a sugar cube in his own way
then mixing it with tea
and closing his eyes.

I've never had tea in Berlin but
I've just unwrapped another sugar cube.
Now I have two sugar cubes. I think of
each one as Berlin. I love them equally.
I hate them equally. I place them
on my bedside table. I drink the tea plain.
In the morning they'll be there.
Two skies rising out of two skylines—
my sweet little Berlins
I can do with as I please.

The Window Poem

I've been a long time
reading a long book
in a long room.

A tall window
above my tall bed
lights the tall pages.

Barbecue and Blood Drive

(Main Fire Station: six a.m. to noon)

What I want to know
is when do you eat—
before, during, or after?

I imagine lying on a cot, a needle in my arm,
someone placing a paper plate with spareribs
on my chest, beginning to wonder
if there will be music, a high school marching band,
a fool with a banjo or conga drums.

And why the fire station?
Why not a hospital or a clinic?
Is there something they aren't telling?
A possibility of a participant catching fire
too close to the barbecue pit?

People waiting in line: relatives of firefighters who
came early to cook, ladies from a church,
a woman who looks lonely, a man who looks mentally ill,
a dozen men and women who have no place to live,
people who can't find work, unemployed parents with
children trading blood for food.

Blood Drive, Blood Drive
then slam it in reverse
Drive Blood, Drive Blood

when blood is the color of fire engines.

II.

Communiqué

The shadow of the sun crosses the desert.
The oasis is covered with land mines.
The mirages are on fire.
A veil of smoke covers the moon.

Which Way

We are passing under bridges made of water
into the ancient future.
A déjà-voodoo tie-dye sky
slides toward night.
The only friends we have left
are our enemies.

The weather vane has gone insane.
North and south are east and west.
Geography is a plot to overthrow itself.
Which way is the floor?
The map is covered with cigarette burns.
Our compass is a pouch of bones.

After the Liberation

The best way to stay alive was to play dead.
Children with Crayola eyes offered homemade bombs.
The wounded were carried on glass stretchers.
Freedom became mandatory.

The sun and the moon disappeared
into the vertical horizon.
Everyone threw their hands into the air
and never brought them down.

Refugees

Families fragmented like grenades.
We fled with only the things we were unable to carry.

Some followed the sun; others, the stars.
Everyone arrived at the same destination
at different locations.

Snow-bones covered the landscape.
Our leaders seemed confused by the alphabet,
remained silent when they spoke.

The Election

The candidates were anonymous; the issues, unknown.
Slogans were wordless.
Protesters marched with blank signs.

Voters were selected by lottery.
Ballot boxes were stuffed with suicide notes.
The results have never been revealed.

Have a Nice Day

The sun is decapitated
from the sky.
It falls and
rolls across the desert.

The executioner holds it up
by its hair of fire.
The photographs are blinding.

Its eyes remain open,
its mouth as if
about to speak.

Empty Canteen

A soldier
holding his helmet

filled with rainwater
drinks his reflection.

Found Poem

It has been reported
that an Iraqi woman
north of Baghdad
told U.S. soldiers
that she would
give information
if they would
kill her husband.

Too Late to Run Out of Time

A flock of jets eclipses the sun.
Migration of migraines.

The enemy is repetition.

Children tell time by gunfire.
The calendar ticks.

Crossing the Desert

The snake and the rock are one.
Everything appears to be another thing.
It is intended that way. It is necessary.
It is a way of saying,
"I am not what you think I am.
I do not feel safe; therefore, I am dangerous."

We have forgotten our destination.
We pass the map back and forth.
We are looking for each other.
I think that I am you and you think
that you are me;
it is the perfect camouflage.

Stop

dragging your heart around
by its tail

leaving its impression
in the sand

making it easy for the enemy
to track.

Across the River

Their dogs
have been set on fire.
Their children
sold into slavery.
Their crops
eaten by soldiers.
Their wells
filled with blood.
Their houses
turned into ash.
Their livestock shot.

The only thing to eat
is a swarm of flies
buzzing back and forth
between the faces of
the dying and the dead.

Red Revolution

If the opera could be infiltrated, order could be restored.
Children were under suspicion for wearing strange colors.
Rallies without people released a mass of emotion.

Some had scissors in their hands, forced others
to kneel down in broken glass.
Some knelt in broken glass by choice.
The only thing worth living for was death.

But before morning came, the river
rose from its bed like a snake and swallowed
the earth like an egg.

Virtual Lack of Reality

The police, dressed like soldiers,
come out of a trapdoor in the bed with
dogs on paper leashes, dogs trained to
detect the odors of coffee and aspirin.

The police strip-search us one by one.
We strip-search the police.
The police strip-search each other.
We strip-search ourselves.

We are arrested for possession of currency.
We are tattooed with handcuffs and barbed wire.
We are sentenced to life without death.
The background music is genetically modified.

Stalking the Predator

The bones of the enemy make adequate crutches.
Our tracks are ahead of us;
the horizon, behind us.
We are followed by children who
ventriloquize us with profanity and prayer.
Our hearts are targets.
We camouflage them with fear.
We keep them in pockets.
We hide them in closets.
We forget where we are.
We rummage through drawers and memories.
We forget what we are looking for.
We can't remember what we are about to say.
Our mouths are open. Our eyes are closed.
We move toward the future.
It's the only thing left to kill.

III.

Today

A fish hatches from a stone.
A lizard leaves tracks that grow hair.
A peacock spreads his fan of cards.
A tiger jumps through the sun.

Do Not Read This Poem Until You Have Finished Reading It

the same way you keep finishing your life
before it's over
deciding your future as if
what lay ahead could be planned
without surprises like
somebody suddenly standing
in a restaurant or a city bus
and singing "Bad Moon on the Rise"
and you can't tell
if it's a man or a woman
and you notice
they're strumming a
sawed-off baseball bat
like a guitar
and all of this
just as you were about to say
please bring us the wine or
ask the bus driver
how many blocks
but you get caught in the beauty
of the singing
and the waiters and the bus driver
move their lips to the lyrics and their
heads to keep time.

The Fly

Not knowing human movement to
a fly would seem slow motion
she chased it room to room.
She swatted a Venetian blind,
a lampshade, her image
in a mirror. When it got
out of reach on the ceiling
she lay down to contemplate
but she wondered if she had left
a boiling pot, she remembered
a doctor's appointment, she
thought about her childhood,
her parents, her marriage,
her children. She started
to cry but there it was
on her knee. She would crush it
against her body to kill it
but it was already across the room,
flying in unpredictable patterns,
its acrobatics so elusive
they became an aerial blueprint
of her mind: faces, places, and numbers
buzzing close but out of reach.

The fly flew back to the ceiling.
She lay down again, thought about
nothing and cried. The fly looked
down through its compound eyes
and saw her as a mosaic.
She didn't wake
until afternoon, too late for

childhood, parents, marriage, children. She stared into the shattered mirror and saw what the fly saw.

Dog

A dog carries her heart in her mouth.
She brings it to her master
as if it were a stick or a ball
to be thrown and fetched.
Each time the master throws it farther.
He throws it across a lake.
The dog dives and swims and
brings it back again; wet and breathless,
she lays it at his feet.
This time the master pays no attention.
His mind has drifted.
He wants to kill something.
Maybe a spider or a bear.
Maybe his mother or father.
Maybe he wants to kill himself.
But his mind drifts again.
Now he wants to love something
or remember something or forget something.
His mind is far away, too far
for even the dog to retrieve. He turns
toward home; she follows, her heart
between her teeth.

Directions

The wind sharpens itself
on a man's face.
A woman brings rain
in wooden bottles.
He gives her a fist
full of flowers.
She eats them
one by one
then exhales petals
that take the shape
of a child.
The child sits
on the man's knees
while the man
tells a story
that he cannot remember.
He is drunk on rain.
The woman
sings a song
that she has never heard.
She is drugged by flowers.
The child wants to know
which way
the world is.
The man points
in one direction;
the woman, another.

Should Be

The sun rises from an apple.
Someone is singing in a language

you haven't quite forgotten.
Sheets are around you like white pythons.

You are almost awake, almost asleep;
you are the way you should be.

Across the street someone eats an apple,
sings a song, and starts a

motorcycle with a single kick.
And so the day will take you

straight into the path of
oncoming fire because

we are sculptures made from smoke and
death requires paperwork.

Who You Are

Why do you still refuse to levitate
even though the law of gravity
has been exposed as a hoax?

You have been lost too long
in the back rooms of the moon.

Fast-forward memory into
rewind future where
laughter lets no mouth close,

where neon nylons and champagne
the color of lipstick
arrive without warning.

Take off your halo of coins
and give yourself a name
that is not a word
then say who you are.

Seems to Exclude

The trees release their leaves
while stone-colored rain
tells its music
to the girl who counts
without using numbers
until she becomes
dizzy on the ledge
then jumps
while pulling pieces of words
from stories
holding themselves
underground in her mind
where high-speed headlights
are photographed
as evidence of manifest destiny
the same way
geography seems to exclude her.

Like a Painting

Today the sun is yellow; the sky,
blue and the grass, the grass
green as grass.

It is a landscape where
you lie down in the shade of
an oak tree and dream of white clouds.

It is a landscape absent of threat:
no snake under a rock, no birds of prey
circling overhead.

Hold this day like a painting
toward the northern light and
memorize the colors because

you will seldom see them.
Most days will be paintings where
the sun is a cockfight; the sky

a machine constructed from
barbed wire, bones, and broken glass
and the grass, the grass

a field of nails where you will
lie down under power lines and
dream of lightning.

Old Friend

Even if
you haven't known why
or where you've gone
I can only hope
that wherever you are
is a place
that didn't expect you,
that you have
caught it off guard.

Memories of a Dog with Blue Eyes

He grabbed his keys,
slammed the mountains behind him, and
drove into the night,
the double-barrel headlights
scanning curves and
bridges toward freeways,
the rear window like a studio prop car
from an old movie,
black-and-white scenes of
New York or Chicago,
a cast of pedestrians disappearing
frame by frame
into the thirties or forties
and ahead of him
the midnight sky buckshot with
north stars,
the radio's dial too bright,
the luminous music deciding his direction,
he could drive forever and
forever could drive him,
his diamond taillights
following his despair.

One Word Worth a Thousand Pictures

Say it. It's on the tip of your tongue.
Heard on the street. Whispered in an ear. Told in a dream.
Lost in a closet or pocket.
You wrote it down on a matchbook. Left it in a taxi.
Look it up. Start by closing your eyes, opening
the dictionary, putting your finger on any word.

Say the word that names you.
Say the word you call your parents.
Say the word you call your child.
Say the word you call your worst enemy.
Say the word that names your greatest fear.
Say the word that most embarrasses you.
Say your first word. Say your last word.

How many pictures do you see now?
Told in a dream. Whispered in an ear. Heard on the street.
Found in the back of a taxi by a stranger.
Left for the next passenger to read. Thrown out the window.
Find it. Lose it. You know what it is. Say it.

Going Farther into the Woods Than the Woods Go

He sits at his table, pours a cup of coffee, and
through the window he sees the same trees hanging around
his house that were there the day before.
He takes a sip and wonders what they will do with their lives.

Will they go with the status quo,
turning white, brown, yellow, green,
provide shelter for birds, shade for hares and foxes,

or will they submit to vines, experiment with moss,
get hooked on fungus, run off with a storm,
drop limbs, cause injury, become nothing but logs,

or will they show ambition, become intimate with famous
architects, become polished floors, stately mantels,
elegant banisters, overhead beams in mansions or cathedrals,

or will they become ordinary tables, unpainted with splinters
like the one where he sits? He pours another cup of coffee,
takes a sip, and wonders what he will do with his own life.

Maybe he should join the trees, stand outside
in the sun and the rain, the wind moving his hair,
turning green, yellow, brown, white,
birds on his outstretched arms,
lambs and wolves asleep at his feet.

White Bears

A polar bear on an island of ice drifts toward the sun.
The bear and the ice are white. The sun is yellow.
The colors of the sea and the sky are not determined.

What is your island?
Can you swim if it melts?
What are you drifting toward?

I once saw a polar bear in a museum;
it was nine feet tall and had glass eyes.
A man killed it for sport;
it had become an educational tool.
Adults asked intelligent questions.
Docents gave intelligent answers.
Children thought it was alive and were terrified.

What terrifies you?
Have you ever killed for sport?
Would you kill yourself for sport?

Polar bears are able to swim over sixty miles.
Female bears protect their cubs from their fathers
who would eat them alive.

Did your father ever eat you alive?

Many colors for the sea and the sky are not determined.
What colors would you choose?